Bearded Dragons for Beginners

Basics of Species Appropriate Husbandry and Care in Your Terrarium

ALINA DARIA

ISBN: 9798545174515

Contents

Introduction

Bearded dragons, whose scientific name is *Pogona*, are native to Australia. They are a genus that belongs to the order of *squamata* and within this to the family of agamas (*agamidae*). Agamas - and thus also the genus of bearded dragons - belong to the iguana family and therefore are lizards!

Bearded dragons are a rather concise genus, as there are only eight different species. It is possible that there are other, as yet undiscovered species, but currently only eight species of bearded dragon are officially recognised. All eight species are native to Australia and have not spread globally - at least not in the wild, as bearded dragons are now kept as popular pets in many countries around the globe.

In the wild in Australia, most species of bearded dragons live mainly in trees and sometimes on or in bushes. They also stay on the ground but spend most of their time on trees. This is called *semiarboricolous.*

However, the species *Pogona henrylawsoni* is the only species that actually lives only on the ground and does not stay on trees and bushes. The seven other species inhabit trees and bushes, with three of the species being very widespread in Australia and inhabiting large areas, and the remaining four species being found only in specific, smaller areas.

Most bearded dragons are quite easy to recognise by the numerous spines that cover almost their entire body. The spines are mainly found on the legs, tail and trunk. They cover the animal's body in "neat rows"; one row of spines is found on the head and one on the flanks. But the most conspicuous row of spines is found on the lower jaw and extends across the throat.

Visually, this can resemble a beard - and gives the pogonas the appropriate name "bearded dragons". The throat with the row of spines, which looks like a beard, is spread out when threatened by enemies and, together with an open mouth, is supposed to act as a deterrent.

The body of the bearded dragon is dorsoventrally flattened - this term comes from anatomy and describes the position or direction of the body. Dorsoventral means that the body is flattened from the back towards the belly. Especially when threatened by enemies, the body is strongly flattened. In addition, the body of the bearded dragon is quite inconspicuously coloured.

Most bearded dragons are greyish or brownish, sometimes with a dark pattern. This makes them rather inconspicuous lizards. At least in the wild this is the case - because nowadays, through selective breeding, more striking colours can also be found, for example shades of red, yellow or even white bearded dragons.

Bearded dragons have a very long tail. It can even make up two thirds of the total size of the animal. The legs, however, are usually quite short.

Most bearded dragons are between 25 and 55 centimetres long (between 10 and 22 inches), but this also depends on the species. We will take a closer look at the eight species in the following chapter.

© *Aix Klusiv*

The Eight Types

As already mentioned in the introduction, wild bearded dragons only live in Australia. At present, eight different species are officially recognised. Not all species are kept as pets in the domestic terrarium; some species are more popular than others and sometimes the export of certain species from Australia is even prohibited.

By far the most popular species of bearded dragons in the domestic terrarium is *pogona vitticeps*. In terms of popularity, it is followed by the *pogona barbata* but also the pogona henrylawsoni.

In the following, we will take a closer look at all eight species, mainly focusing on the popular pet species!

1. Pogona Vitticeps:

Other names for the popular Pogona Vitticeps are "Central Bearded Dragon" or "Inland Bearded Dragon".

While "Pogona" stands for the genus of bearded dragons in all species, "vitticeps" is a compound term from Latin. The second part of the word ("ceps") is derived from the Latin term "cephalus", which means "head". The first part of the word ("vitti") comes from the also Latin term "vittatus". This means "striped".

Pogona Vitticeps is the most popular species of bearded dragons worldwide, as it is considered easy to care for. In addition, it is said to be more robust against diseases than other species and therefore better able to ward off pathogens. The beard (i.e., the row of jaw spines) is less pronounced than in the Pogona barbata, but in any case, clearly present. Further rows of spines are found above the eardrum, around the corners of the mouth, on the back of the head and on the sides of the body - left and right to the tail. Pogona vitticeps are very strongly built and have rather short legs. The ventral scales and part of the dorsal scales are keeled (= not smooth).

In the wild, this species inhabits large parts of Australia and is found in numerous areas in both South Australia and Central Australia. However, Pogona vitticeps are also frequently found in eastern Australia. The distribution areas include South Australia, New South Wales, Victoria, Queensland, Northern Territory and several others.

Pogona vitticeps are quite large specimens, reaching a head-torso length of about 25 centimetres (10 inches). The tail length can be up to about 30 centimetres (12 inches). The average total length of the animal is thus about 55 centimetres (22 inches). Most specimens of this species weigh between about 300 and

temperatures or the mood of the animal changes. The inside of the mouth is yellow.

The Pogona barbata is robust and strong. Its body is also flattened, and the legs are also short, like those of the Pogona vitticeps. The head is quite elongated and appears triangular from above. The size of the Pogona barbata is similar to that of the Pogonas vitticeps, as it also has a head-torso length of about 25 centimetres (10 inches). The tail, however, is somewhat longer; it is about 30 to 40 centimetres long (12 to 16 inches). One thus arrives at a total length of the animal of about 55 to 60 centimetres (22 to 26 inches).

3. Pogona Henrylawsoni:

Pogona Henrylawsoni are also called "Lawsons Bearded Dragons" or "Rankins Bearded Dragons".

They are the only species of bearded dragon that live solely on the ground and not on trees - unlike the other species, Pogona Henrylawsoni are therefore not arboricolous.

As ground dwellers, Pogona henrylawsoni mainly inhabit grasslands, at best semi-deserts with a grass cover. These areas are called "Black Soil Plains". There are no trees here, only the so-called Mitchell Grass.

This type of grass is only found in Australia. Although there are no trees in this area and the animals live on the ground, they certainly use elevated places for sunbathing and climb on rocks, for example.

Their distribution area is in Central Australia, more precisely in the north-east of Central Australia. They are found almost exclusively in Queensland.

Their name comes from the Australian poet and philosopher Henry Lawson, after whom this species was named!

Pogona henrylawsoni are quite small. They reach a total length of about 30 centimetres (12 inches), with just under half of this length being accounted for by the tail. The head-torso length is therefore only about 15 centimetres on average (6 inches). In other respects, too, the typical features are less pronounced than in the other bearded dragon species; for example, they have fewer spines. The spines, especially the beard, are not as strongly developed as the beards of the other species and the head appears rather stocky. In addition, Pogona henrylawsoni have fewer lamellae and fewer preanal pores than the other species.

The colouration of Pogona henrylawsoni is yellowish, brownish or sometimes olive. In addition, two rows of pale spots run from the nape of the neck over the body to the end of the trunk.

In the home terrarium, however, the Pogona henrylawsoni can reach the same age as the other species. There are quite a few Pogona henrylawsoni that also lived to be 15 years old. It is also one of the three most popular species in the domestic terrarium.

Pogona Henrylawsoni – © Teefarm

4. Pogona Minor:

This species is often also called "Dwarf Bearded Dragon".

The scientific name of the western bearded dragon is Pogona minor ("minor" = "small"), as it also belongs to the smaller bearded dragons.

Pogona minor colonise the area from Western Australia to Central Australia in the wild. They can also be found on some islands, such as Barrow or Dirk Hartog. Their tail is usually longer than the body. The head-torso length averages about 15 centimetres (6 inches).

The tail is about 22 to 25 centimetres long (9 to 10 inches), so that the Pogona Minor is usually 37 to 40 centimetres long in total (15 to 16 inches). It is thus larger than Pogona henrylawsoni, but still significantly smaller than the other species.

This species also has spines on its body, but these are far less pronounced than in the other species. Pogona minor do not have a "proper beard", but spiny scales on the neck. Unlike the other species, Pogona Minor also cannot erect the "beard". There are also spiny scales on the head, but all of them are less pronounced than in the other species.

The colouration is greyish/brownish. There are also several light spots on the body. The neck is usually darker than the body and the ventral side is lighter. The inside of the mouth is usually yellow, although in bred specimens the inside of the mouth is usually bright red.

5. Pogona Microlepidota:

The Pogona Microlepidota, which is often called "Small Scaled Bearded Dragon" or "Drysdale River Bearded Dragon", is native to north-western Australia – especially to Kimberley.

Kimberley is a region in the state of Western Australia. The Kimberley region is located within this state in the northwest and borders water to the north and west.

However, the Pogona Microlepidota is not found in domestic terrariums (outside Australia) - at least it should not be found there, because export from Australia is strictly prohibited!

This species has some similarities with the Pogona minor, as it also cannot spread its beard and the body size is also very similar. The body grows to an average length of about 40 centimetres (16 inches), although about two thirds of this length is accounted for by the tail. The torso is therefore quite short, and the head is also rather small and narrow.

The colouration of this species is brownish - mostly greyish-brown or yellowish-brown. The ventral side is lighter than the rest of the body. This species does not

Island and East Wallabi Island. Unfortunately, the Pogona Minima is classified as an endangered species.

For a bearded dragon, Pogona minima has rather long legs and is also rather slender compared to the sometimes quite broad and sturdy bearded dragons. The name does justice to this species, because the Pogona minima has a total size of only about 35 centimetres (14 inches), of which usually even 24 centimetres (9.5 inches) are allotted to the tail. This species also has no "real beard" and no continuous rows of spines around the entire neck, but only spines in the rear jaw areas. On the rest of the body, too, there are only three more, rather undeveloped rows of spines.

© *Bernhard Rohm*

Single Housing, Groups and Socialisation

Wild bearded dragons are solitary animals that are very rarely found in loose associations. It is probably more by chance that bearded dragons are found in the same area in the wild. As a rule, bearded dragons live strictly alone! At mating time, males and females naturally come together. They reproduce, but do not start a family, but go their separate ways again after mating.

Accordingly, pet shops often give wrong advice, because in many cases the customer is told that a bearded dragon has to live in a group. This is wrong. The most species-appropriate husbandry is single keeping. Nevertheless, keeping a bearded dragon in a group may work under certain circumstances - but there is never a guarantee for this so keeping them in groups is not recommended.

Under no circumstances should two male bearded dragons be kept together! The males are extremely dominant and defend their territory very aggressively if other males intrude. The fight does not necessarily start immediately on the first day, but sooner or later there will definitely be a fight between the two males. Both will be extremely stressed and also suffer psychologically from the unnatural situation.

In the wild, no male will accept another male in his territory, but in a terrarium, they cannot avoid each other and see the only solution in a fight. In the worst case, this can end with the death of the inferior animal. The animals can bite off limbs and tails or otherwise seriously injure each other.

© *Claudia Nass*

If you absolutely want to keep several bearded dragons together, the only option is a group of females or a harem. Harem keeping means that a male is kept together with several females. A female does not represent a rival for the male, but it can happen that the male presses a single female too much and the female becomes psychologically extremely stressed. If you keep a male with several females, a single female does not have to "carry the load alone". However, it should also be noted that only females that are at least two years old can live in a harem. The male encourages the females to lay more eggs, and this is very exhausting, especially for young animals! It is also possible that the male chooses a favourite female and predominantly mates with her. Many problems can occur so keeping a bearded dragon as a single is always better and not as stressful for the animal.

In pure female groups there is less danger of the animals quarrelling and fighting, but females also have their individual characters, which do not always fit together. Females usually tolerate each other, but the danger of a fight always exists. Even after many years. Therefore, keeping them individually is recommended.

There is no guarantee that the group members will get along in the long run. This is also a question of character because each animal has its own individual personality. Unfortunately, it often happens that even after years of peaceful coexistence, a group still quarrels and sometimes seriously injures each other. In this case, each animal must have its own terrarium! It is not in the nature of the bearded dragon to live together with several animals in a small space for a long time.

If you want to "play it safe", it is better to get only one bearded dragon! This corresponds best to the natural way of life.

However, if you decide against keeping them individually and opt for a harem, you will inevitably have to ask yourself what to do with the fertilised eggs. In principle, breeding belongs in the hands of very experienced bearded dragon owners who have several years of experience to show.

In principle, a layperson and beginners should not breed. Successful breeding requires background knowledge - also regarding genetics - and a lot of responsibility must be assumed.

Castration is neither sensible nor possible for bearded dragons (or reptiles in general). Thus, mating will inevitably occur in mixed groups.

Therefore, some keepers decide to take the fertilised eggs out of the terrarium after egg laying and freeze them. After freezing, the eggs are disposed of. If this method is chosen, the eggs must not be disposed of immediately. Freezing is imperative to prevent little babies from developing in the egg if it has already been discarded!

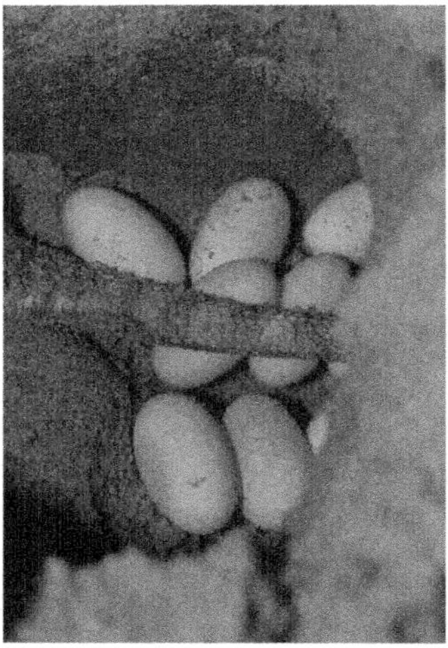

Bearded dragon eggs

If you cannot ethically justify this or do not want to go to this extra trouble, it is best to keep only one female OR one male in single housing. Keeping them singly is the safest form of husbandry anyway, and also the least stressful for the bearded dragon. Furthermore, keeping them singly prevents fights, which can happen suddenly at any time - even if bearded dragons have been living peacefully together for years.

So far, so good. And can bearded dragons be socialised with other animal species? The simple answer is: No. On the one hand, other animal species have completely different habitat requirements. On the other hand, they cannot communicate with each other properly. Often there are fights, one animal sees the other animal as prey, etc.

In the past, some keepers had the idea of socialising bearded dragons with geckos. This is not recommended at all, as the two species need different living conditions, which cannot be achieved at the same time anyway! If you want to keep both reptiles, you need two or more terrariums.

Genders

Gender determination in reptiles can often be quite difficult. In general, it is not only somewhat more complicated to determine the gender of bearded dragons, but also of most other reptiles and amphibians. With mammals, this determination is much easier, even for a layperson.

With young animals, determining the gender is still impossible and can only be realised when the animal is a little older and mature, because the genital organs only become more pronounced in the course of time. Therefore, a reliable determination is only possible after a few months.

Baby bearded dragon.

Male bearded dragons can raise their beard very wide (if they belong to one of the species concerned, see chapter "The eight types") and often also turn the tip of their tail black. Through these gestures they threaten their rivals. Female bearded dragons are usually not as good at threatening, for example their beard does not spread as much as the beard of the males. In addition, the spines on the head are usually larger and more imposing than those of females, also to threaten male rivals. However, the gender cannot be clearly determined by these characteristics because they can vary and be differently pronounced. A clear gender determination is therefore only possible by looking at the genital organs of the bearded dragon.

The males have two hemipenis pouches and also femoral pores. The femoral pores are found on the inner thighs and form rows there. The femoral pores are glands, but sometimes they can also be quite pronounced in females. Therefore, the observation of the femoral pores only serves to support the already established result and cannot serve as the sole method of identification.

But what is it about the hemipenis pouches of males? The term "Hemi" comes from ancient Greek and means "half". The term "Hemipenis" therefore means something like "half penis". This term is used to describe the male genital organ or mating organ of squamata. Since bearded dragons belong to the squamata, this also applies to them.

However, bearded dragons do not have hemipenis pouches exclusively; they are also found in other species of squamata, such as geckos for example.

The hemipenis pouches are located on the sides of the cloaca. They are bulging pouches, each of which contains a hemipenis. Sometimes the hemipenis pouches are also located below the cloaca at the base of the tail. However, this is not the rule.

The hemipenis pouches with the respective hemipenis form quite early, whereas the femoral pores usually form later.

The females, on the other hand, have a clitoral pouch. This is located above the cloaca. So, we note:

- ✓ The male has two (!) hemipenis pouches

  → lateral next to the cloaca

  → shape: elongated

- ✓ The female has one (!) clitoral pocket

  → above the cloaca

  → shape: trapezoidal

If you want to look at the genital organ, you should never simply turn the bearded dragon onto its back. A much gentler and more pleasant method is to let the bearded dragon sit on its four legs and only guide the tail carefully upwards. The tail is lifted gently and slowly until the genital organ becomes visible.

For better identification, the cloacal area can be shone through with a torch. Hold a torch on this area from above. From below, it is usually easier to determine the gender, because if you hold the torch at the right angle, you can see either the trapezoidal gender organ of the female above the cloaca or the elongated hemipenes (=plural of hemipenis) of the male to the right and left of the cloaca.

Pogona vitticeps.

Purchasing Bearded Dragons

If one wants to acquire pets, many people almost automatically turn to a conventional pet shop. However, pet shops unfortunately often give the wrong advice, as the staff are often not specially trained in reptiles. This is not only the case with reptiles such as bearded dragons, but also with other popular pets such as rodents, amphibians, fish, etc. Therefore, it is advisable to at least take the information from pet shops with a grain of salt.

Furthermore, pet shops often sell animals that are not ready to be given away - some animals are injured, some animals are sick, some animals are still too young. It will usually be difficult for a layperson to judge whether an animal is ready to be given away.

It is therefore more advisable to buy reptiles such as bearded dragons from a reputable breeder. Reputable breeders either concentrate on one specific species of bearded dragon or on only a few different species of bearded dragon. This allows them to gain a lot of experience and they are experts in their respective field. When they hand them over, the animals must be healthy, must not have any injuries and they must be old enough. It is not necessary for a bearded dragon to be fully grown when it is surrendered, but it must at least have reached its surrender weight.

A reputable breeder will pay attention to all these aspects and give the new owner comprehensive advice. Serious breeders attach great importance to the fact that their animals come to beautiful and species-appropriate homes and are therefore also happy to answer open questions. The animal will also be prepared for transport.

Of course, it is also possible to take bearded dragons from a reptile care centre or second-hand. Care centres are often privately owned, but animal shelters also have bearded dragons from time to time. Taking on a second-hand bearded dragon because it is no longer wanted in its old home is also a commendable decision. However, there is a risk of unintentionally taking on a sick animal that would be better off in expert hands until it is healthy again.

The Terrarium

Domesticated bearded dragons are kept in a terrarium at home. And they need space! Although there are no legally binding regulations regarding the minimum size and equipment of the terrarium, the bearded dragon community has meanwhile established quite sensible minimum dimensions and "furnishing" recommendations, which are based on many years of experience and help to set up the terrarium as species-appropriate as possible. The focus here is on trying to recreate the living conditions in the wild as closely as possible.

The absolute minimum dimensions of a terrarium are generally 150 centimetres in length (60 inches), 80 centimetres in width (30 inches) and 80 centimetres in height (30 inches). These dimensions should never be undercut, as otherwise the bearded dragon would have to live in far too confined a space. The dimensions 150 x 80 x 80 centimetres (60 x 30 x 30 inches) are the minimum dimensions for one (!) bearded dragon.

Not recommended, but: if two bearded dragons are kept, the terrarium should be at least 180 x 80 x 80 centimetres (70 x 30 x 30 inches). For each additional bearded dragon, 20 centimetres (8 inches) should be added per animal.

Nevertheless, the following always applies: the more space, the better for the animal! If you have the possibility, you should provide the bearded dragon with a terrarium that is two metres long (80 inches long). Life in a confined terrarium is of course not comparable to life in the wild, where the animals can move freely. Therefore, the above specifications are only minimum dimensions that should be met in any case. Those who can provide a larger terrarium should definitely do so, as bearded dragons enjoy plenty of space.

These measurements may differ from what has been read or heard so far. On 10 January 1997, the Federal Ministry of Food and Agriculture published a report by the expert group on the minimum requirements for keeping reptiles.

This states the basic formula "4 x 3 x 2" for the minimum size of the terrarium. This formula is multiplied by the head-torso length of the reptile. The tail length is not considered in this formula.

For example, if you have a Pogona vitticeps with a head-torso length of 10 inches, the minimum dimensions for the terrarium are: 4*10 x 3*10 x 2*10. According to the recommendation of the Federal Ministry, the terrarium should therefore have the dimensions 40 x 30 x 20 inches.

This may have been acceptable almost 25 years ago in 1997 and may have been appropriate to the state of knowledge at that time, but today it is generally known that bearded dragons simply need a lot more space. This formula is not applicable to almost any reptile, as virtually all reptiles require more space than the formula calculates.

Once the perfect terrarium has been bought or built, the question naturally arises as to where it should be placed in the house. In any case, you should make sure that the terrarium is not exposed to direct sunlight, as terrariums can heat up very quickly. Often this is not noticed in time and the animal may suffer a heat shock, even if it is used to quite high temperatures due to its Australian origin. Furthermore, the terrarium should not be placed directly next to a heater, as the terrarium temperature can be controlled better if it is not influenced by a heater.

In addition, the terrarium should not be placed directly on the floor, but elevated. Whether you use a TV cabinet, a sturdy chest of drawers, an aquarium stone base, a self-built structure or similar as a shelter is an individual decision. However, the shelter should be able to withstand the weight of the terrarium permanently. The elevated position prevents cold from the floor. This often also helps to avoid draughts. In addition, the terrarium can be better observed when it is elevated.

The terrarium should be in a rather quiet place. Bearded dragons are diurnal and therefore usually awake when humans are awake. When humans are asleep, the bearded dragon sleeps at about the same time. Therefore, the day-night rhythm of bearded dragons does not have to be considered as much as that of geckos, for example, because most (!) gecko species are nocturnal.

Nevertheless, bearded dragons can be stressed by too loud noises. Of course, it doesn't have to be as quiet as a mouse, because reptiles also get used to a certain background noise and to the sounds that can usually be heard in their home. Nevertheless, these noises should not be so loud that the bearded dragon gets scared and frightened.

Furthermore, a good air exchange should be ensured in the terrarium. Many terrariums already have a ventilation system included. To prevent the air from accumulating and to ensure that the air exchange works well, the vents should be placed at least on two opposite sides. Nevertheless, not too much warm air should be able to escape from the terrarium. In addition, the insects to be fed should not be able to "escape" from the vents.

The topic of "substrate" is a contentious issue for many reptiles and is discussed very controversially. When choosing the substrate, one should consider from which area the respective reptile originates and what the substrate normally looks like in this area.

The substrate for bearded dragons should be firm, but also capable of digging. In addition, it should be sunk quite high. Many keepers and breeders in Germany therefore opt for a mixture of sand and clay. Sand alone would be too loose and would not provide any support! This would also be bad for the animal's joints. Clay alone is often considered to be too firm and not suitable for digging. If the soil is not suitable for digging, a female may have difficulty laying eggs, for example, because she may not be able to find a suitable place to lay them. However, loose substrate is not only bad for the joints but also for the digestion of the animal as they often swallow a bit of the loose substrate when eating – and this can result in (sometimes severe) digestion problems.

In English speaking countries, owners and breeders also avoid loose substrate such as sand for the above mentioned reasons (joints, digestion). Clay is often used as well, however, in English speaking countries you can find a bigger variety of substrates. Other suitable substrates therefore include:

- Tiles

- Reptile carpet / bearded dragon carpet

- Rubber shelf liners

However, if you use the above mentioned options you need to make sure that a female bearded dragon still has suitable places available to lay her eggs.

In Germany, the combination of sand and clay provides a suitable mixture for recreating a species-appropriate substrate as closely as possible. The ratio is approximately 3:1 (3 parts sand to 1 part clay). Such a mixture can either be bought or mixed yourself. Terrarium sand as well as fine building sand, fine play sand or fine bird sand are suitable.

Then mix the sand with the clay powder in the ratio mentioned above - four parts sand to one part clay. The dry mixture is then enriched with water and needs some time to dry. Depending on the weather and temperature, drying can take a few days. In the terrarium, the substrate should then be about 10 to 15 centimetres high (4 to 6 inches). Please make sure that the substrate is not loose but rather firm.

An extremely important aspect is the lighting and heat in the terrarium. Reptiles do not regulate their body temperature independently, but through their environment. Therefore, they are all the more dependent on being exposed to species-appropriate temperatures and being able to switch between different zones as needed.

In the terrarium, the bearded dragon should have different heat zones available so that it can switch between these zones and regulate its temperature. Three areas are ideal: The normal environment, plus sunny areas and additional shaded areas. The shaded areas are of course the coolest places. The shaded areas should have a temperature of about 25°C to 28°C (77°F to 82°F). The sunbathing areas should have a temperature of about 45°C to 50°C (113°F to 122°F). For the remaining areas, i.e., for the normal ambient temperature, about 30°C to 35°C is appropriate (86°F to 95°F).

To achieve these temperatures and to regulate them, lighting is essential. In addition to normal lighting, special heat lamps should be purchased to warm the sunbathing areas.

The lighting in the terrarium should be switched on for twelve hours every day - ideally always at the same times, for example from nine in the morning to nine in the evening every day. If the bearded dragon is in brumation or is being led in or out, the lighting duration will vary and deviate from the twelve hours that are the normal standard.

Metal vapour lamps and infrared light should not be used, as they can cause injuries and burns on the skin. The eyes of the bearded dragon could also be injured. Halogen lamps with reflector inserts are more suitable. UVB light is also popular, as it also helps the animals to produce the vital vitamin D3 - which is actually a hormone.

The humidity in the terrarium should be about 40% during the day and about 60% at night. The exact level is rarely achieved, but these percentages should be roughly aimed for.

A night light is not necessary, however. After all, bearded dragons are used to darkness and need it for their day-night rhythm so as not to get confused. However, it is advisable not to close opaque blinds completely so that moonlight can shine into the room and twilight can also be experienced.

In any case, the bearded dragon should have some hiding places available. Many bearded dragons only come to rest completely in a hiding place, because they feel safe there. Care should be taken to ensure that the hiding places are large enough for the bearded dragon to fit into comfortably. The openings must also be large enough so that the animal does not get stuck and/or hurt itself. However, the hiding places should not be too large either, so that the bearded dragon has a good view of it and can feel secure.

What to use as a hiding place is an individual decision. There are no limits to creativity - of course, sharp edges, pointed corners and similar risks of injury should be avoided. For example, you can use caves made of cork or bark, halved flowerpots, stone structures, large roots or cork oak bark.

Many keepers also provide their bearded dragons with a so-called "wet box". This is common practice with many reptiles, for example geckos, snakes etc. Wetboxes are caves or plastic boxes lined with damp moss, in which the humidity is extremely high - they are like tiny wet biotopes. Here, the reptiles can fill up on moisture. Sometimes wet boxes are also lined with moist coconut fibre humus, which works just as well as moist moss. Wet boxes are not compulsory and not all bearded dragon owners or reptile owners use them, but they do have some advantages. The extremely high humidity in the wetbox facilitates and supports the moulting of the reptile, it keeps the skin nice and moist, is sometimes used as an egg-laying place and can prevent skin diseases if necessary. For hygienic reasons and to avoid mould, the inside of the wetbox should be replaced about once a week. Besides the wetbox, however, other dry hiding places should be offered.

In the hiding places, the bearded dragon comes to rest, but when it is awake, it enjoys a few opportunities to occupy itself. Therefore, you can offer the bearded dragon climbing opportunities such as thick, rough branches. Of course, these should be stable so that they do not topple over or wobble too much. This could injure the bearded dragon.

© *Gerhard G.*

The back wall of the terrarium should also offer opportunities for climbing. With a plateau back wall, several elevations and platforms can be integrated into the back wall so that the bearded dragon can use them as storage places and for climbing. In order for the bearded dragon to be able to climb well on the back wall, the wall including the plateaus should be made of rough material. A back wall with platforms also offers the advantage that the bearded dragon can use them not only for climbing and depositing, but also as shady spots and viewing platforms for looking over the territory.

Heat-resistant plants can also be integrated well into the bearded dragon terrarium. Plants should not be completely omitted, as they provide a pleasant climate in the terrarium and regulate the humidity. On the one hand, the selected plants must be able to cope with the high temperatures in the terrarium and, on the other hand, they must not be poisonous, as bearded dragons like to chew on the plants or eat them whole. Golliwoog is a well-suited plant for bearded dragon terrariums, which is also eaten with pleasure. Other well-suited plant species that are not poisonous but are still rather rarely eaten and are therefore well-suited for the bearded dragon terrarium include:

Tillandsia, Lithops, Echeveria, Beaucarnea Recurvata and Gasteria.

What do we need for a species-appropriate terrarium?

Let's summarise all the important points in a checklist ...

- ✓ terrarium - minimum dimensions!
- ✓ suitable place in the house
- ✓ good air exchange in the terrarium
- ✓ suitable substrate, e.g., sand/clay mixture
- ✓ correct temperatures incl. sunny and shady areas
- ✓ lighting, 12 hours a day

- ✓ good humidity
- ✓ several hiding places, including a wetbox if necessary
- ✓ climbing facilities (branches, back wall, ...)
- ✓ plants, e.g., Golliwoog, Tillandsia, Gasteria, ...
- ✓ at least one water bowl, preferably several (fresh water daily)
- ✓ food bowl(s)

Diet and Nutrition

Animals are roughly divided into carnivores, herbivores, frugivores and omnivores. These upper categories are often subdivided into further subcategories. For example, insectivores belong to the carnivores and leaf-eaters belong to the herbivores.

Bearded dragons belong to the omnivores. They consume both animal proteins in the form of insects plus plant food. The main part of the diet should consist of plants.

In the wild, the bearded dragon is responsible for finding its own food. In addition, it moves around more in the wild than in a terrarium at home. But at home, the food is handed to it by the owner - therefore domesticated bearded dragons are not used to managing their food intake on their own.

For this reason, the owner is responsible for selecting and rationing species-appropriate food. It is sometimes observed that domesticated bearded dragons have difficulty developing a sense of satiety and eat more food than they need - if it is offered to them. Therefore, humans must take care that the bearded dragon neither becomes too thin nor too fat. Overweight is generally quite widespread in pets and there are also sometimes obese bearded dragons.

Excess weight can lead to various diseases in the long run. In this respect, animals are no different from humans, as many diseases in humans are also triggered or supported by obesity. Excess weight and obesity are one of the most frequent causes of death in pets.

Adult bearded dragons should be fed according to the formula 80:20 - 80% plant food and 20% animal food in the form of live insects.

It is best to offer an adult bearded dragon living insects once or twice a week. The bearded dragon should not be given more than four insects in total per week. Of course, the animal always needs access to fresh plant food. We'll get to this a bit later.

The most suitable (animal protein) bearded dragon food is live ...

... crickets

... cockroaches

... and grasshoppers.

Cockroaches and grasshoppers are preferable to crickets, as cockroaches and grasshoppers are more nutritious and therefore healthier.

Mealworms are very high in energy and therefore contain many calories. Therefore, mealworms should - if at all! - only rarely be offered as a snack.

The weight of the bearded dragon should always be kept in mind. Many bearded dragon owners feed their animal twice a week with two food animals each time or once a week with three food animals at once. Both options are fine.

The insects can be fed live or dead. However, there are countries where live feeding - even of insects - is not permitted by law. In Germany for example, live feeding is not prohibited in principle, but is handled much more strictly when feeding vertebrates than when feeding invertebrates.

The interests of the hunter are opposed to the interests of the prey animal. On the one hand, some species, such as the bearded dragon, are natural hunters and have a hunting instinct that they should be able to act out.

However, it should be noted that bearded dragons are so-called "lurking hunters". They do not actively hunt and do not pursue their prey ("chasers") but remain patiently in one place and wait for prey. When a prey animal comes by, the bearded dragon snaps at it.

On the other hand, prey animals also have rights and, as a matter of principle, they must not be harmed without good reason. In Germany, for example, it is now forbidden to feed live mice to snakes. There are only a few exceptions to this ban.

The requirements for feeding live insects are not as strict because insects are invertebrates. Feeding them to bearded dragons, for example, is therefore permitted, but the prey animals must also be cared for appropriately and must not suffer unnecessarily or be mistreated.

Whether to feed live insects is therefore also an ethical question. Most bearded dragon owners feed their insects in live form, as this allows bearded dragons to live out their hunting instinct and as this is most similar to the diet in the wild. Bearded dragons are not scavengers.

To simulate that a dead insect is still alive, there are so-called vibration feeding stations. In many cases, however, these do not serve their purpose, as most bearded dragons can tell whether the insect is still alive or already dead. These devices are usually a waste of money.

Furthermore, living insects contain important nutrients for the bearded dragon, which are often lost with dead insects.

Whether the insects are placed in the terrarium with tweezers or offered in a food bowl is an individual decision. In any case, the bearded dragon should not be disturbed and stressed too often by humans.

One could get the idea of looking for insects for the bearded dragon in the wild. However, whether this is advisable is highly controversial. On the one hand, bearded dragons do not eat many insects and not very often - so it actually makes little or no difference to the wallet whether you collect food for the bearded dragon in nature or not. The financial aspects are negligible, also because many insect species can be grown / bred quite easily at home. This minimises the risk of pathogens or harmful substances.

In addition, collected food from nature offers no added value compared to purchased or home-grown fresh food. The critters from the wild are no better or more nutritious than the purchased food, as long as they are alive or fresh.

Personally, I see no advantage in collecting insects and other foods from the wild. However, I do see some disadvantages and dangers.

Live food can introduce parasites and other pathogens into the bearded dragon's terrarium. With an omnivorous animal like the bearded dragon, the danger of this is always greater than with an herbivorous animal like guinea pigs or rabbits because parasites often use insects as intermediate hosts on which they nest for a while.

If food with pathogens is introduced into the terrarium, these pathogens and parasites will pass on to the bearded dragon quite quickly and use it as a host.

Of course, this is also possible if the food is bought or home-bred. As a rule, such a risk cannot be ruled out. However, the risk is higher if the food is collected in the wild.

Other toxins could also be accidentally introduced into the terrarium if the food is obtained from the wild. Here, of course, it depends in which areas and on which land is collected. Pesticides, rat poisons and other harmful substances pose a real risk, which can be avoided if the food is bought fresh or even home-grown.

Of course, bearded dragons also need to drink enough - water is the be-all and end-all for a healthy animal. Therefore, bearded dragons should always have water available so that they can drink at any time of the day or night when they feel thirsty. The water bowl should be cleaned regularly, but without chemical cleaners. Simple vinegar has an antibacterial effect and is wonderful for cleaning.

80% of the diet for an adult bearded dragon should consist of plant food. In 1974 and 1975, the stomachs of a total of 18 wild bearded dragons were examined and the ratio of animal to plant food was recorded *(Richard E. MacMillan, Michael L. Augee & Beverly A. Ellis; Thermal ecology and diet of some xerophilous lizards from western New South Wales; Journal of Arid Environments (1989) 16, 193-201).*

Juveniles eat more insects than adults. The study also included three juvenile bearded dragons. In their stomachs, the proportion of animal food was 52% and the proportion of plant food 48%. Thus, young animals feed approximately half on plants and half on animal protein.

Juvenile © Ramirez

Domesticated young animals should therefore still be offered insects as food almost daily. This is slowly reduced when the young animal is three months old. Until then, young animals should be fed about three times a day. After the third month, the amount is reduced bit by bit until the animal is one year old. From then on, it is fed according to the rules for adult animals. Of course, young animals are also given plant food every day.

Adult bearded dragons eat much less animal food. The main component of their diet is plant food. Even bearded dragons that consumed an above-average amount of insects still ate more than two-thirds plant food.

As a rule, the percentage of plant food is even higher in adults. On average, it is at least 90%, and even bearded dragons have been studied whose stomach contents consisted of 96% plant food and only 4% animal food. Of course, it always depends on where exactly the animal lives and what food sources are available. The rule 80:20 is therefore not a rigid guideline but can vary.

When feeding plants, however, fruit, legumes, nuts and tuberous vegetables should be avoided. The bearded dragon should be fed mainly "green food", i.e., lettuce, leaves and (wild) herbs. This leafy food is very rich in crude fibre, which is essential for the bearded dragon's digestion.

Fruits, tuberous vegetables and similar plant foods can throw the digestion out of balance and cause diarrhoea. The bearded dragon's digestion is designed for leafy foods that are very rich in crude fibre. This is because bearded dragons come from areas where they do not find fruits and vegetables, but rather leafy plants with a high raw fibre content. Feeding high-sugar and/or high-calorie fruits and vegetables can also lead to faulty fermentation in the digestive tract and excessive proliferation of intestinal parasites.

In addition, many bearded dragon owners also set aside one fasting day per week. This is not compulsory but helps to relieve and cleanse the intestines.

Which vegetable food can be offered to the bearded dragon?

… Lettuce

- ✓ Lollo Rosso
- ✓ Endive lettuce
- ✓ Romaine lettuce
- ✓ Radicchio
- ✓ Chicory
- ✓ Rocket (although strictly speaking rocket is a type of cabbage)

... Leaves

- ✓ Kohlrabi leaves
- ✓ Carrot greens
- ✓ Radish greens
- ✓ Hazelnut leaves
- ✓ Apple tree leaves

... Wild Herbs

- ✓ Dandelion
- ✓ Daisy
- ✓ Nettle
- ✓ Clover
- ✓ Goutweed
- ✓ Ribwort and common plantain
- ✓ Bedstraw
- ✓ St. John's wort
- ✓ Chickweed

✓ Camomile

✓ Margarites

✓ Speedwell

✓ Cranesbill

<u>… Kitchen Herbs</u>

✓ Basil

✓ Dill

✓ Cress

✓ Oregano

✓ Rosemary

✓ Thyme

✓ Sage

✓ Peppermint

It is important to ensure that the diet is varied. Of course, it is not necessary to offer a new type of green food every day, but you should make sure that the bearded dragon is always offered some alternatives, has a choice and always has enough plant food available.

Supplements

Domesticated bearded dragons living in a home terrarium run the risk of suffering from nutrient deficiencies. Therefore, most breeders and owners supplement various minerals and vitamins to provide the bearded dragon with everything it needs for a healthy life.

But why is this so? In the wild, bearded dragons not only eat insects, leaves and other plant food, but they also specifically look for food that meets their nutritional needs. For example, they sometimes find sources of various minerals on the ground. Furthermore, animals in the wild get enough vitamin D3 - which is strictly speaking a hormone but is called a vitamin - through direct sunlight on the body. In the terrarium, this is only given to a limited extent if, for example, special UVB fluorescent tubes are used. The substrate in the terrarium also does not provide any added value for covering some essential nutrients.

Furthermore, the nutrient supply also depends on what the insects are fed with, which the bearded dragons then eat. If the insects are fed a very one-sided and poor diet, they will naturally not contain all the important nutrients that they could ultimately pass on to the bearded dragons. If you do not breed the insects yourself, it is quite difficult to check how nutritious the purchased insect actually is. Plant food is easier to control.

But which nutrients are particularly important? Calcium is an extremely important mineral for bearded dragons and almost always needs to be supplemented. Otherwise, there is a risk of calcium deficiency (hypocalcaemia), or the animals could develop rickets (bone disease; soft and/or bent bones).

Since calcium is so important for the bones, among other things for their construction and stability, calcium should always be freely available to the bearded dragons. Often a small bowl of calcium powder is permanently offered to the animals in the terrarium. Especially young animals and pregnant females need this for healthy growth and/or egg production, but adult bearded dragons are also very dependent on a sufficient calcium supply. A large proportion of bearded dragon breeders and owners resort to cuttlebone powder (or ground cuttlebone shells) for calcium supply. This comes from the cuttlefish and in most cases smells accordingly strong.

Therefore, it must be mentioned that not all bearded dragons like cuttlefish powder and consume it. Sometimes the grated cuttlebone is not offered in a small bowl but scattered directly in the terrarium. In pet shops it can often be found with the bird food. If a bearded dragon does not accept the cuttlebone powder, there are many other odourless calcium powders on the market.

The calcium powder should be offered in a cooler corner of the terrarium and ideally not near the drinking water. It should also be checked regularly to see if the calcium powder has already been used up and/or if there are droppings in the bowl.

Calcium powders are divided into calcium citrate and calcium carbonate. Calcium citrate is artificially produced, whereas calcium carbonate is obtained from a naturally occurring source. Therefore, calcium carbonate usually has about four to five times the amount of calcium.

In addition, bearded dragons have an increased vitamin D3 requirement, even though they can use UVB radiation. Vitamin D3 is important for the health of all living creatures. Furthermore, the supplemented calcium cannot be permanently stored in the bones if there is a vitamin D3 deficiency. For this reason, a vitamin powder should be supplemented that also contains vitamin D3. This vitamin powder can, for example, be sprinkled over the insects to be fed before feeding. It is usually sufficient if the vitamin powder is given every second feeding.

But magnesium and vitamin K are also important for the correct utilisation of vitamin D3 and calcium. Therefore, magnesium and vitamin K should also be found in the vitamin powder.

Brumation

Wild bearded dragons keep a brumation and often in the wild the brumation is taken over the summer months - for example from June to August. In Australia, July is the coldest month of the year!

Brumation should be distinguished from hibernation! Some mammals keep a strict hibernation, during which they actually sleep deeply and shut down completely for the duration. Brumation differs from this because the bearded dragon does not sleep completely and continuously, but instead shows a very reduced activity - it just comes to rest for a while. This is not a cold torpor, as is often the case with snakes or amphibians.

During brumation, the bearded dragon's metabolism slows down and its heart beats more slowly. However, bearded dragons are not completely motionless during brumation, but move from time to time, for example to drink. Therefore, they always need fresh water.

So why do they go into brumation? Brumation is very beneficial for the health of the bearded dragon and usually life is prolonged. The body has time to regenerate and recover.

In many cases, domesticated bearded dragons also initiate brumation on their own. When this happens varies greatly. Some bearded dragons want to go into brumation as early as September, some not until December. In most cases, brumation is initiated when the light conditions become darker, and the temperature becomes cooler. Slowly they eat less, become quieter and are generally less active. Brumation begins when the days become shorter, the temperatures decrease, and it slowly gets darker.

However, it is important that only healthy bearded dragons are "sent" into brumation. Sick animals should not be kept in brumation. Sometimes illnesses cannot be detected immediately, so the bearded dragon should be checked for general health and parasites before starting brumation. At the very least, a faecal sample should be submitted to a laboratory for examination. If parasites are detected, the animal should not go into brumation, as this can cause the parasites to multiply even more and radically worsen the situation.

At the beginning of the brumation, the feeding of the bearded dragon is stopped. The bearded dragon then excretes the food remains that are still in its body. This is important because otherwise the food in the abdomen could start to rot while the bearded dragon is in brumation.

About two weeks after the last feeding, start reducing the lighting time. It is advisable to first reduce the lighting time from twelve to ten hours. Then reduce the lighting time by three hours every week - to seven hours, to four hours, to one hour. Once you have reached this point, all light sources and heat sources are switched off. Some bearded dragon owners use a different rhythm and reduce the lighting by half an hour every day. Both variations are fine.

Whether the bearded dragon then spends the brumation in the terrarium or in a quarantine box is an individual decision. This also depends on where the terrarium is located in the house or flat. If the room is too warm and/or too bright, the bearded dragon should definitely be moved to a cool and dark place during brumation. The temperature should be around 15°C (60°F) during brumation. This temperature should not be seriously exceeded or undercut, so that the metabolism for the brumation mode is not abandoned. A cellar is usually wonderfully suitable for this.

As the bearded dragon only rests and does not sleep continuously, it still needs drinking water and a hiding place. The drinking water should continue to be changed daily, but apart from the necessary water change; the animal should not be disturbed in its rest.

Brumation lasts about three to four months in total. As a rule, the animals do not lose any (or hardly any) weight during this time. However, if they visibly lose weight, the brumation should be stopped. A weight loss of about 10% is still ok.

After brumation, it is important that the bearded dragon is only slowly re-acclimatised to warmer temperatures and more light. The steps that were taken to bring the bearded dragon into brumation are now repeated in reverse order. The lighting time is slowly increased, and the temperatures slowly become warmer. Only when normal conditions are reached again, the bearded dragon is fed again. Before the first feeding, the bearded dragon should have been living under "normal" conditions again for about seven to fourteen days - i.e., a lighting duration of twelve hours and normal temperatures.

© *Yann Ferlaak*

Behaviour

The behaviours of reptiles in general and bearded dragons in particular sometimes differ considerably from the behaviours of other animals or humans. Therefore, many gestures are often misinterpreted. The following is a brief overview of common bearded dragon behaviours in order to avoid misinterpretations in the future and to interpret the behaviour correctly.

Pogona Vitticeps – © Harald Matern

- <u>Lying on top of each other:</u>

Presumably it is meant to confuse attackers like birds of prey when bearded dragons lie on top of each other. This makes them appear larger and not as defenceless as a single bearded dragon. Often, they are mistaken for carrion because they are lying on top of each other and are therefore not attacked. Another theory is that bearded dragons also want to regulate their body temperature by lying on top of each other.

© *Bojoux*

- Climbing on the arm:

Bearded dragons have no need to cuddle or to be close to humans. If they climb onto humans, it is usually because they want to climb to a higher position so that they can observe better from there.

- Eye closure:

When a bearded dragon closes its eyes, this is very often misinterpreted. Closing the eyes is not a sign that a bearded dragon is comfortable, but rather a sign of rejection. The bearded dragon does not feel comfortable and fears danger. This often occurs when the owner strokes the animal. By closing the eyes, the owner thinks the bearded dragon likes the petting - but the opposite is the case. Bearded dragons are not cuddly animals.

- Putting up the beard:

Bearded dragons put up their beard to threaten enemies and opponents. Usually, the mouth is opened wide at the same time to appear even more threatening.

- Ducking:

When a bearded dragon ducks, it wants to appease its opponent. It is not looking for a fight but shows humility before the opponent. This is to prevent a fight.

- Dark colouration:

The dark colouring of the body usually enables the bearded dragon to absorb heat better and more efficiently. Once the animal has absorbed enough heat, the body usually turns lighter again. But it can also happen that only the beard turns dark. This happens either because the bearded dragon is not feeling well, because it wants to threaten an enemy or simply during mating season.

- Hissing:

When a bearded dragon hisses, it is threatening its opponent. It is in fight mode.

- Cuddling:

Bearded dragons do not cuddle. If they snuggle up to humans, it is because they are trying to raise their body temperature by doing so. Bearded dragons belong in their terrarium and should only be taken out in emergencies.

- Licking:

Bearded dragons investigate their environment by licking it. Both furniture and food and any other bearded dragons are licked. This transmits scent to the so-called Jacobson's organ. This is an olfactory organ in many animals.

- Opening the mouth:

Bearded dragons sometimes open their mouths when they are too warm. This allows them to cool down a bit, as the moisture in the mouth can escape and evaporate. But also when they have an opponent in front of them and want to threaten him, bearded dragons often open their mouths. At the same time, they spread their beard to appear threatening.

- <u>Nodding:</u>

Nodding the head is a sign of dominance. It also supports the other threatening gestures like spreading the beard. However, nodding also takes place during courtship behaviour and is accordingly not a threatening gesture during mating season.

- <u>Flattening:</u>

Flattening is a protective function against predators, primarily birds of prey.

- <u>Glass scratching:</u>

Sometimes bearded dragons scratch at the glass of the terrarium because they do not understand why they cannot pass through, even though the glass is transparent. Some bearded dragons do not understand that glass is a barrier, especially when they are young and inexperienced. But scratching can also be a sign that the bearded dragon is not comfortable in the terrarium and is trying to break out - perhaps the terrarium is too small, the temperature is not right, etc.

- <u>Waving:</u>

Waving the arm is meant to appease the opponent. It is a similar sign to ducking. If the bearded dragon waves its arm, it is not looking for a fight and shows humility before its opponent. The bearded dragon recognises that the other bearded dragon is the higher-ranking animal.

© Reinhart Zehetbauer

Common Diseases

Everyone gets sick sometimes. Some more often, others less often. Even reptiles like bearded dragons are not immune to diseases, and the severity ranges from "very mild" to "potentially fatal". But how often and how severely a bearded dragon falls ill can be determined to a large extent. As with humans, prevention is the be-all and end-all - a bearded dragon that is kept in a species-appropriate manner, whose needs are met and which receives a balanced and healthy diet, will very rarely become ill. Of course, certain diseases can occur even if an animal is kept under perfect conditions, for example through heredity or just plain bad luck. However, over 90% of diseases in reptiles are caused by humans - not intentionally, but mostly through simple ignorance of the optimal husbandry conditions.

Among the most common mistakes regarding husbandry and nutrition are, for example ...

... too much dryness in the terrarium

... overfeeding (leading to excess weight)

... no brumation

... stress (e.g., due to lack of space and/or incorrect group constellations; e.g., one stressed female on two males, etc.)

... fear (e.g., due to too few hiding places)

... too high or too low temperatures

It is not always necessary to visit the vet for every little ailment. A visit to the vet is always associated with stress because the bearded dragon is torn away from its familiar environment and has to face a very stressful and strenuous situation, which can sometimes even take several hours, including the journey.

Nevertheless, for liability reasons, I will not recommend any self-treatment or self-medication. Beginners in particular may misjudge and treat diseases incorrectly, as they do not have much experience with bearded dragons. Accordingly, I would like to point out that diseases must always be identified and professionally treated by a competent veterinarian.

When choosing a vet, make sure that the person chosen has experience with reptiles. This is an absolute must. Reptiles are so fundamentally different from other pets such as rodents, dogs, cats etc. that a reptile cannot be treated by just any vet. A reputable vet will only treat a bearded dragon anyway if they feel confident to do so based on their experience and can treat the animal professionally.

In some areas it can be quite difficult to find a vet who is well versed in reptiles. This varies from region to region. It is possible that a fairly long journey will have to be accepted. A long journey is of course more stressful for the animal, but it is better than having the animal treated by a vet who does not know reptiles well and may make mistakes. Therefore, it is a good idea to start looking for a suitable vet at an early stage in order to have the right contact person at hand immediately in case of an emergency.

Of course, the owner must be sensitised to the recognition of diseases. If you know your animals, you will notice quite quickly if something is wrong and if an animal changes. Not every little change has to be a sign of a disease, but the following signs often indicate diseases - especially if they occur in a combination ...

... loss of appetite, refusal of food

... sudden aggressiveness and irritability

... unnatural movements

... changes in the shape, colour and/or consistency of the faeces

... loss of joy of movement

... discolouration of the skin

Although a disease is a case for the vet, the owner should be able to recognise the different diseases in principle. Therefore, we will now take a closer look at some common bearded dragon diseases.

1. Abscesses

Abscesses are collections of pus that are caused by bacteria. In principle, an abscess can occur in any part of the body. Usually, an abscess is caused by an external injury, for example, a cut on a sharp object. Bacteria can now enter the animal's body through the open wound and possibly cause an infectious abscess. When reptiles get an abscess, however, the pus inside is usually not liquid, but encapsulated and quite hard. In the worst case, the bursting of the abscess can lead to blood poisoning if the germs enter the bloodstream through it, and the animal can even die. Therefore, many abscesses have to be removed surgically. Whether surgery is necessary and what treatment is appropriate will be decided by a competent veterinarian.

2. Intestinal parasites

Parasites are basically divided into ectoparasites and endoparasites. Ectoparasites are "external living" parasites, for example mites on the skin. Endoparasites are "inside-living" parasites. Intestinal parasites are therefore classified as endoparasites. They include tapeworms, coccidia, hexamites and the like. Almost all animals are infested by parasites sooner or later and this is usually easily treatable. However, artificially created habitats - for example, in terrariums - will increase infestations quite quickly if they are not recognised and treated early, because there is not much space available in the terrarium. How strong or weak the parasite infestation is often also strongly depends on the animal's psyche. Stress, fear and other negative emotions weaken the animal's immune system and thus its defences. If an animal is infested with intestinal parasites, this can usually be recognised quite easily from the faeces. The consistency of the faeces becomes soft and resembles mush, and in acute infestation there is often severe diarrhoea. Sometimes even worms can be seen on the faeces; however, this is not always the case. In addition, the diseased animal often loses weight (sometimes rapidly), even with good nutrition.

3. Diarrhoea

As we noted earlier, intestinal parasites can cause diarrhoea. However, diarrhoea is not always due to a parasite infestation. There are many possible causes of diarrhoea. Since diarrhoea can sometimes dehydrate an animal very quickly, it is important to identify the cause of the faecal change. The dehydration of the body also affects the kidney function, causes a loss of electrolytes and can lead to further intestinal diseases. Diarrhoea is defined not only as watery faeces, but also as mucousy and very soft faeces. There is a particularly urgent need for action if there is even pus and/or blood in the faeces. A specialist veterinarian must be consulted immediately.

Besides intestinal parasites, the following factors can also cause diarrhoea ...

... stress and other psychological strains

... spoiled food

... fruit / sugar

... changing the food too quickly

... overfeeding or malnutrition

... medication

... diseases of the liver or gall bladder

... toxins

4. Moulting problems

As reptiles grow throughout their lives, they shed their skin regularly. A healthy and species-appropriate bearded dragon has no problems with moulting and does it without complications. However, if an animal has moulting problems, the moult either fails completely or certain parts of the skin do not detach from the body. In the worst case, moulting problems can strangulate smaller parts of the body because they can no longer be supplied with blood well - this mainly affects the tip of the tail and the toes. In most cases, moulting problems are due to insufficient humidity in the terrarium. Conditions that are too dry sometimes make moulting immensely difficult. Furthermore, bearded dragons often support their moulting by rubbing the "old" skin on objects such as stones. If the animal has no possibility to rub off the skin, problems often occur as well. Other diseases such as dehydration or infections can also make moulting difficult, but too dry conditions and lack of opportunities to rub the skin are the two most common causes of problems. Particularly in the winter months, the air humidity sometimes drops extremely, so it is important to ensure that the air humidity is sufficiently high, especially in the colder months.

5. Heat stroke

Especially in summer, you should make sure that it does not get too hot in the terrarium. Depending on the terrarium, heat can sometimes build up, especially if the terrarium is too small and/or does not have enough ventilation. Therefore, you should keep a close eye on the temperatures during the hot months. Even if heating mats or similar devices are used, overheating can sometimes occur. It is also particularly risky if the terrarium is exposed to direct sunlight - then the temperature can rise extremely within a very short time. If it is too hot, heat stroke can be imminent, although bearded dragons in the wild in Australia are used to high temperatures. In the worst case, this can even lead to death. The animals often become lethargic and restless, sometimes even suffering locomotor disorders or foaming at the mouth. They try to cool down, but this is often not possible within the confines of the terrarium. If an animal suffers a heat stroke, it should be taken out of the terrarium immediately and moved to a cooler place. The animal should be stabilised by a cool bath or cool wet cloths. However, make sure that the water is not too cold! You want to stabilise the temperature quickly but cooling too brutally can cause shock. In addition, the animal must now drink a lot of water. However, a bearded dragon should not suffer heat stroke in the first place.

6. Liver diseases

Liver disease is quite common in reptiles when the liver is permanently overloaded due to poor housing conditions. The liver is a detoxification organ and also needs a break now and then. An unhealthy lifestyle puts too much strain on the liver, and it cannot recover from its work. Therefore, liver diseases are usually caused when an animal is fed too often on a permanent basis and/or is given food that is too high in calories. People sometimes mean too well for the animal and overfeed it. However, this is detrimental to health, as bearded dragons simply have a different nutritional rhythm than, for example, humans or other popular pets. A lack of brumation can also lead to liver diseases or diseases of other organs, as the body has plenty of time to recover and regenerate during brumation. Liver disease tends to develop slowly, so there are usually no symptoms at first. At a later stage, the urine and faeces of the sick animal often become discoloured and take on an unnatural colour.

7. Egg binding

When females have problems laying eggs, this is called egg binding. The eggs may either not be laid at all or only partially, they may block the cloaca and/or the oviduct, cause a prolapse and in the worst case may even rot in the animal's body. In the case of acute egg binding that is not treated in time, the animal may even die - for example, from blood poisoning or kidney failure. The blockages can lead to bloated bellies, cramps, refusal to eat and the like. It can occur, for example, if a female is not encouraged to lay eggs. However, it may also occur if there are no suitable places to lay eggs. In addition, deficiencies such as vitamin D3 deficiency are often a reason for egg binding. In order to prevent it, a sufficient supply of all necessary vitamins and minerals should always be taken care of. Also, egg-laying places should not be lacking. If egg binding nevertheless occurs, a veterinarian experienced in reptiles should be consulted as soon as possible.

8. Mouth rot (stomatitis)

Stomatitis is an infection in the mouth of the animal. In the bearded dragon, however, stomatitis usually occurs less frequently than in other reptiles, such as turtles or snakes. Stomatitis often develops as a result of other infections in the body or parasite infestations. General metabolic disorders can also trigger the disease. If the oral mucosa is injured, stomatitis has an easy time. If there is also a wound in the mouth, this can also lead to a bacterial infection. In the worst case, stomatitis can even cause blood poisoning and abscesses can form. The sick animal often dehydrates quite quickly and often refuses food.

9. Mites

Mites are parasites that - unlike worms, for example - do not live inside the animal but on the skin. Therefore, they are often visible from the outside, but this is not always the case. The more severe the infestation, the more likely it is that even a layperson can recognise a mite infestation. Mites like to nest in "corners", so they mainly infest the cloaca, the corners of the mouth, the bends of the joints and similar parts of the body. Mites cause itching, so affected bearded dragons usually rub themselves on objects to relieve the itching. The stronger the immune system, the better the animals cope with mites. If the immune system is not particularly good anyway, for example due to an unhealthy diet or stress, the animal suffers particularly badly from the infestation. As a rule, a mite infestation must be treated with appropriate medication, which the expert veterinarian will prescribe. It is also important to clean the terrarium thoroughly and replace the substrate to prevent a new infestation after treatment.

10. Kidney diseases

Kidney disease, like liver disease, is quite common in reptiles. Similar to the liver, the kidneys also take care of detoxifying the body. The kidneys act as a toxin filter for the body, and they remove germs and other pathogens. If the kidneys are diseased, the urine is usually discoloured, too dark, somewhat slimy or too cloudy. Like liver diseases, kidney diseases develop rather slowly and insidiously, but they are almost always triggered by incorrect husbandry conditions. For healthy kidneys, sufficient fluid intake is the be-all and end-all. Therefore, it is essential that the animals always have enough fresh water available. If an animal is dehydrated or does not drink enough water, this can lead to severe damage to the kidneys in the long run. But hypothermia can also lead to kidney damage over time. Therefore, always make sure that the temperature zones are appropriate.

11. Rickets

Rickets is also often called **metabolic bone disease**. It is a disease of the bones caused by a permanent calcium deficiency. A calcium deficiency is also called hypocalcaemia. Sufficient calcium intake - in combination with vitamins D3 and K and magnesium - is essential and absolutely necessary for a healthy and stable skeleton. In rickets, there is reduced bone density and a change in bone composition. Especially young animals and pregnant females have an increased need for the aforementioned micronutrients. Damage is usually very difficult or impossible to heal. If an animal has rickets, the bones become soft and deformed. Deformities can occur and the bones can thicken in certain places. Rickets can cause secondary diseases, because the affected animal often has restrictions of the musculoskeletal system, suffers from calcifications and kidney diseases, sometimes has problems eating due to deformed jaws and much more. Females may also suffer from egg binding. It is therefore important to prevent rickets from occurring in the first place - by providing sufficient essential micronutrients.

12. Excess weight

If a bearded dragon suffers from excess weight, this is almost always due to poor husbandry. Usually this is simply because the animal is fed too often and/or too much. In the wild, you will hardly find an overweight animal, because there the animals take care of finding food themselves, generally move more and regulate their food intake better themselves. All this is omitted when keeping animals at home and the human is responsible for selecting and regulating the food for the animal. Excess weight can - as in humans - cause many other diseases and is often the reason for fatty liver, kidney diseases, rickets, etc.

Dear reader: For independent authors, product reviews are the basis for the success of a book. Therefore, we depend on your reviews. This not only helps the authors, but of course also future readers and the animals. Therefore, I would be extremely grateful for a little review on this book. Thank you very much!

I wish you all the best, much joy with your bearded dragon and the best of health!

Legal Notice

Author: Alina Daria Djavidrad

Contact: Wahlerstraße 1, 40472 Düsseldorf, Germany.

1st edition (2021)

© *Gerhard G.*

© *Justine Doc*

Room for Notes

Printed in Great Britain
by Amazon

73665239R00075